Lexcel Business Continuity Planning Toolkit

Related titles from Law Society Publishing:

Lexcel Client Care Toolkit (2nd edn)
The Law Society

Lexcel Financial Management and Business Planning Toolkit
The Law Society

Lexcel Information Management Toolkit
The Law Society

Lexcel People Management Toolkit
The Law Society

Lexcel Risk Management Toolkit
The Law Society

All books from Law Society Publishing can be ordered through good bookshops or direct from our distributors, Prolog, by telephone 0870 850 1422 or e-mail **lawsociety@prolog.uk.com**. Please confirm the price before ordering.

For further information or a catalogue, please contact our editorial and marketing office by e-mail **publishing@lawsociety.org.uk**.

Lexcel Business Continuity Planning Toolkit

The Law Society

The Law Society

ISBN 978-1-85328-751-0

Published in 2011 by the Law Society
113 Chancery Lane, London WC2A 1PL

Typeset by Columns Design XML Ltd, Reading
Printed by Hobbs the Printers Ltd, Totton, Hants

The paper used for the text pages of this book is FSC certified. FSC (the Forest Stewardship Council) is an international network to promote responsible management of the world's forests.

Contents

Preface

Business continuity planning is an essential management activity for any size or type of organisation. Effective planning can help identify, mitigate or manage factors that could negatively impact the access to your workplace and provision of services to clients.

The *Lexcel Business Continuity Planning Toolkit* is designed to help practices identify, plan and manage areas of risk in this area. The Toolkit is intended to be a practical starting point which practices can use to support their own business continuity planning. The emphasis is on covering the factors and impacts in the context of a legal practice. The Toolkit includes outlines of strategic, operational and regulatory factors, how to plan, and guidance on recognised methodologies.

The toolkit also provides a wide range of templates including:

- Business continuity project outline plan
- Business continuity awareness training statement
- Risk and dispersal matrices
- Business continuity plan
- Emergency evacuation procedure
- Incident form template/log sheet
- Exercise self-assessment tool
- Master events list

We hope that you will find the Toolkit useful both as a reference guide and as a practical resource in your day-to-day work.

The Lexcel Office would like to thank Chris Needham-Bennett MSc MBCI, the managing director of risk and business continuity consultancy Needhams 1834 Ltd, based in London. Chris has worked in business continuity since 1996; clients of Needhams 1834 Ltd include several international law firms as well as medical research organisations, data companies, national parliaments and banks. His interest in risk and business continuity stems from his previous military service in the Parachute Regiment, work on Home Office-sponsored private finance initiatives and his academic study on the psychology of risk taking and effective planning.

We would also like to extend thanks to two of his current colleagues, Richard Fitzhugh and Philip Russell, and three former colleagues, Giles Alexander, Tim Catt and Patrick Roberts.

The Lexcel Office
The Law Society

1 Introduction

1.1 Why plan?

Business continuity might be something of an alien subject to many and, as in any project, an understanding of the origins and drivers behind the rise to prominence of the concept is useful for the person responsible for its introduction into the firm or its ongoing development.

1.2 The history of business continuity

Business continuity arguably began with the rise of the criticality of IT systems in businesses. Often in the earlier days business continuity planning was almost exclusive to the IT department and was a mystic art shrouded in acronyms.

As hardware and software became increasingly resilient the focus of business continuity broadened to include the vital people element. The realisation that staff members are indeed the practice's most valuable asset was slow to evolve but that asset is now the accepted priority in business continuity planning.

More recently the broader concept of risk and its management, together with a societal preoccupation with risk and media focus on the topic have engendered regulatory and compliance demands that have propelled business continuity on to senior management agendas.

1.3 Pressures for business continuity

Practices are institutions on which clients depend, and clients' expectations are high. These high expectations also include the clients' perception that the practice will always be available to deal with their matters, hence the need for good business continuity plans. This is echoed in a raft of regulatory advice which is commented on in the body of the work.

Naturally one cannot ignore the fact that a practice is normally or should be a profit-making concern. Even an in-house legal department within an organisation should be cost effective. Therefore, the speedy resumption of business that is facilitated by a good business continuity plan not only ensures ongoing profitability but also has the potential to enhance the reputation of the practice; an example is the speedy recovery of a top 100 practice following a series of unfortunate events including a bombing.

If, however, an incident is responded to poorly, the reputational penalty can be damaging or even fatal to a practice of any size. The recent examples of BP,

Barings, Société Générale and others illustrate the point, whereas the Virgin Rail crash at Carlisle was, despite a tragic fatality, well handled and did little to damage the Virgin brand.

Additionally, many practices deal with highly regulated clients such as banks, financial institutions and ordinary companies. Often clients will reflect their own regulatory pressures on their suppliers of services. Increasingly, tenders require formal reassurance as to the continuity plans of suppliers, even to the point of requiring sight of a firm's continuity plan.

1.4 Good practice

In an attempt to establish best practice in business continuity the British Standards Institute developed British Standard 25999. This is designed to be an auditable standard of business continuity which reassures clients as to the practice's resilience. While BS 25999 seems a step too far for most practices, its process and methodology are probably the most advanced. Therefore, this toolkit is based on alignment to BS 25999 and the requirements of Lexcel v4.1. There are some references to BS 25999 parts 1 and 2 to assist the reader.

1.5 Benefits of business continuity

Until very recently there was no concrete evidence that any insurer (underwriter or broker) would offer reduced premiums in recognition of a good business continuity plan. Now the author is aware of two large multi-site practices that have been given considerable reductions in premiums based on the efficacy of their plans. Largely the reductions are founded on recognition that the plans will reduce the downstream consequential losses caused by issues which would otherwise not have been identified and remedied and for which the insurers would otherwise incur costs.

1.6 Responsibilities

Requirement 2.3(d) of the Lexcel standard states that there must be a person responsible for the plan. The person to be appointed to create or control a business continuity plan is important in so far as they have to have the confidence of the managing partner or the equivalent. It does not really matter if they are the practice manager in a small firm or the national Head of Facilities of an international firm; the critical issue is the support of the executive for the project.

Hopefully this introduction has offered some materials to the reader who may have to convince colleagues of the need for the investment of time, money and effort to achieve a robust and proven business continuity plan.

1.7 Layout of the toolkit

Each chapter of the toolkit has sets of documentation to support the chapter. These are by analogy and necessity the 'plain vanilla' style of documentation. Practices will probably wish to tailor the tables and charts to their own situation, adding columns and detail as appropriate. So long as the basics are right, the rest will follow.

Each chapter is complete in its own right and can be read in isolation or as a linear process. If a reader is familiar with the topic in a particular chapter the next chapter is where the next stage begins.

Some case studies are included at **Chapter 8**. They are there to illustrate some critical points as opposed to being instructional in their own right; the lessons are very specific.

1.8 Some top tips before you start

One of the problems you will face irrespective of the size of the practice is the allocation of effort or labour to each phase of the project. In terms of importance and where concentration of effort should be placed the following advice is offered.

1.8.1 Risk assessments

Risk assessments and risk registers are vital and a requirement of the Lexcel standard, but only in so far as they lead to some risk mitigation and can be referenced to some planned response. One can argue that almost every major town and city in the UK has a similar risk profile. Remember that terrorist bombs are not a London issue alone. Such events have occurred in Exeter, Birmingham, Warrington and Guildford within the author's memory. A large aircraft crash in a populated area last occurred in the UK at Lockerbie. Statistically a firm is more likely to be impacted by hardware failure so keep a sense of perspective in risk assessments.

1.8.2 Business impact analysis

In terms of building the plan, the business impact analysis (BIA) is vital; it is really the 'brain' of the plan. Therefore in terms of effort it is essential that this element is correct and agreed within the practice, and that plans are based closely on the results. It will take longer than will be first thought and is an iterative process needing constant review as circumstances change.

1.8.3 The plan

A current business continuity debate within the profession concerns the level of detail required in the plan. We suggest small 'lightweight' departmental checklists are preferable and more likely to be used than a mighty tome of plans. By all means keep detail in available annexes, but bear in mind user friendliness and portability. It is essential that the staff, both legal and support, contribute to plan authorship.

1.8.4   Training and exercising

There is little point in having a fantastic plan if it remains unknown to the potential users. Requirement 2.3(e) of the Lexcel standard stipulates that practices must have a procedure to test the plan at least annually. Exercises and training have to be made dynamic, interesting and relevant. As a rough rule of thumb, authorship and delivery of an exercise will take twice as long as is anticipated at the outset. Do not skimp on this issue; what you rehearse will largely be what happens in reality.

1.9   Definitions, myths and distinctions

There is a lot of talk and debate about semantics. As you become more familiar with business continuity planning you will undoubtedly hear these debates aired. It is useful to be familiar with the debate.

- The government and local authorities tend to talk about 'resilience', meaning the continuation of essential services in the face of adverse conditions.
- Recovery centres tend to talk about 'disaster recovery' (DR) implying that if you need to use their centres or sites you must have had a disaster.
- Public relations agencies often dwell on 'crisis management', such as a product recall of food because of contamination.
- The 'blue light' services (the police, fire and ambulance services) tend to talk about 'emergency response' because this is the part of an incident with which they are likely to deal.
- Businesses usually talk about 'business continuity', meaning the continuation of services to clients in the context of a practice.

However, all the disciplines are usually interrelated. Any or all of them have some bearing on business continuity. A brief example illustrates the point:

> The practice has a fire in the building. The fire service puts it out and the document store in the basement is flooded (emergency response). The staff move to a disaster recovery site (disaster recovery). The managing partner makes a statement to the press as to the 'resilience' of the practice and that normal service will be maintained to clients (crisis management). Meanwhile the staff retrieve the documents from the basement and operate client services from the recovery site (business continuity).

2 Planning the project: what to do before you start

Ideally the business continuity plan should be approached like any other project. Naturally, different practices will have their own methodologies. However, there are certain common features which include:

- senior management buy-in to the project;
- setting a budget;
- setting a timeframe; and
- publicising the project internally to the company.

2.1 Senior management buy-in to the project

Senior management need to understand the need for business continuity plans as they are likely to be the group approving the expenditure on behalf of the practice. Unless your practice has had a major incident recently, you will probably have to persuade them of the benefits of a robust plan. Hopefully one or two of these drivers will strike a chord with the senior management team.

2.2 Regulatory and compliance

The first driver for buy-in is the regulatory requirements to have some form of continuity plan. The two main sources are quoted below.

- Requirement 2.3 of the Lexcel standard states that:

  Practices will have a business continuity plan, which must include:

  (a) an evaluation of potential risks and the likelihood of their impact
  (b) ways to reduce, avoid and transfer the risks
  (c) key people relevant to the implementation of the plan
  (d) the person responsible for the plan
  (e) a procedure to test the plan annually, to verify that it would be effective in the event of a business interruption.

- The Solicitors' Code of Conduct 2007, rule 5.01(1)(k) requires provision for 'the continuation of the practice of the firm in the event of absences and emergencies, with the minimum interruption to clients' business'. Under the new outcomes-focused regulation, risk management is covered in Principle 8 and Chapter 7 of the draft SRA Code of Conduct refers to business continuity specifically (indicative behaviour 7.3).

There are a number of additional drivers related to other issues, which are outlined below.

2.2.1 Insurance costs

More and more insurance companies are offering reduced premiums if their clients have well-developed continuity plans. This is because the plans potentially reduce their downstream consequential losses. Premium reductions are significant with one major practice achieving a high six-figure year on year premium reduction.

2.2.2 Tender processes

Under the Civil Contingencies Act 2004 many central and local government agencies and the emergency services have to maintain their own business continuity plans. Their procurement staff have now incorporated questions in tenders to potential suppliers concerning their continuity plans so as to ensure a resilient supply chain. Likewise, banks and other financial institutions ask similar questions of their potential suppliers to comply with their regulatory demands.

2.2.3 Communications

It is important that the interests of all staff in the continuation of the business are safeguarded.

2.2.4 The practice's other policies

Most practices will maintain policies on equality and diversity and health and safety. The ideal is to make a comparison with business continuity and these well-established policies.

2.3 Gaining buy-in from key staff

There are usually five key staff whose 'buy-in' is critical to the success of a project; they are not always the most senior staff but they are influential. It could be the senior PA who represents secretarial staff or it might be the IT manager. Practices should try to include a representative from each department, unit or team to ensure engagement across the practice.

One of the first steps in creating your business continuity plan is to identify and engage with these key members of staff. **Annex 2A** can be of use in this process:

- List five key staff members who would be critical to have 'on board' in any business continuity project or the development of existing plans.
- What would their main objection be to the project and what argument would you use to overcome their objection?

Meeting with all five staff members at the same time is often more productive because all are involved in the debate. In such a meeting you will find support for different aspects of the project from different people so it is not just you advocating the project and you will be more likely to succeed.

2.4 Setting a budget

It is very difficult to set an accurate budget as axiomatically one does not know at this stage exactly what one will find that will require remedial actions. However, one can anticipate the following features will need to be addressed and the costs will be roughly in proportion to the size and complexity of the practice:

- improvements to the IT systems, their resilience and speed of recovery;
- purchase of disaster recovery site space;
- possible consultancy support;
- possible audit fees;
- possible purchase of an automated call cascade system to keep staff informed of events;
- remote access to databases, such as CITRIX or VPN;
- improvements to home-working facilities and IT security;
- management time for interviews, training and exercising; and
- your own time diverted away from your own core activities, if you are not the business continuity manager.

2.5 Setting a timeframe for the project

> **Note:** It is always worth including some contingency days for unforeseen events and changes during the project.

The timeframe for a project of this nature will vary only according to the size of the practice. Nevertheless certain features, as outlined in the table at **Annex 2B**, will remain common to all projects.

The table at **Annex 2B** is based on an assumption that the project is to be completed in six months. In order to use the table for your own practice, you will need to make suitable adjustments to the number of days allocated to each activity. Practices should consider the implications for their resources, in particular when setting realistic key milestones.

Please note that some activities can be commenced before the preceding activity is completely finished; others in the earlier stages are more likely to be sequential.

2.6 Publicising the project internally

It is vital that all staff are aware of and, more importantly, understand their role in the business continuity process. A template letter to staff from the managing partner or equivalent (**Annex 2C**) and an outline project plan (**Annex 2D**) are offered as examples. Practices should consider the most appropriate method to communicate this to their own staff.

Annex 2A
Key staff

No.	Name and title	Objection	Argument for BCP
1			
2			
3			
4			
5			
Comments and notes to self:			

Annex 2B
Project plan table

Months	1	2	3	4	5	6
Description of activity						
Scoping	4					
Risk assessment	4					
Business impact analysis		12				
Review of options		2				
Plan authorship			40			
Training of staff				14		
Scenario walk through					10	
Review of plans					6	
Authorship of confirmatory exercise					20	
Confirmatory exercise						10
Exercise debrief and review						8
Contingency days	6					
Total						126

Annex 2C
Template letter to staff

Dear Colleagues

[*Practice name*] has obligations to both our employees and clients. One of these obligations is to ensure that the practice can survive any major operational disruption to [any of] our site[s], thereby preserving our client services and reputation.

To ensure that this is the case we are embarking on a business continuity project and review to ensure that our practice is competent and capable in this area and that our staff and clients can have every confidence in our business resilience.

This project will necessitate enthusiastic commitment from you all; everyone has a part to play.

[*Name*] is working on this project and I would like you to make the time to work with [him/her] on this task which has the potential to safeguard all our interests now and in the future.

Attached [*or give details of where plan can be found, e.g. Intranet*] is a very simple version of the project plan which indicates the phases that will be undertaken between now and [*insert month when the project is due to end*].

If you have any questions or require clarification on the project please direct enquiries to [*name*] on [*telephone/e-mail*].

Yours,

[*Name*]

Annex 2D

Business continuity project outline plan

Month	Activity	Commitment or requirements
March/April	Preliminary work on risk analysis of sites within the scope of the project	Materials required: • Locations and maps • Previous incident history • Local authority risk register • Turnover by location • Profit by location • IT infrastructure.
	Setting of interview dates with key staff in all locations	Arrangements to be made by [name].
	Review of current plans	Plans to be provided by [name].
	Review of IT systems and dependencies	IT architecture to be provided by [name].
	Drafting of specific questionnaires and templates	
May	Business impact analysis	Interviews with key staff approx one hour per representative. In this phase [name] will meet with key staff in all locations from all business and support units and examine the critical systems and what impact their loss would entail. The criteria are usually loss of profitability/income or consequent loss.
June	Strategy determination	Following these interviews, the whole of the company is graphed on spreadsheets thereby enabling a strategic overview of priorities to be determined.
	Plan authorship	Following the determination of priorities and strategies, plans will be drawn up in conjunction with departmental heads of legal and support functions in the various locations. This will probably take up to two hours per person per location and might be done as an iterative process involving the exchange of plans in draft format.
July	Approval of plans	After the plans are completed they will be submitted for approval and integrated into the disaster recovery site system for the firm as well as being promulgated internally.
August onwards	Training and exercising of the plans	It is envisaged that the period between August and October will be a training and rehearsal period leading to a large-scale but simple rehearsal of the integrated plan in November.

3 Policies, strategies, assumptions and scope

3.1 What are you trying to achieve?

It is the case in most practices that the existing management structures are there to serve a specific or general strategy. In the same fashion, unless you determine business continuity strategies and policies the resultant plan will be unclear as to its intentions and will therefore be inappropriate for its task.

The stages of this phase are:

- defining the scope of business continuity by intent and geography;
- determining the strategies and supporting policies; and
- making planning assumptions.

3.2 Scope

It has to be determined what the scope of the project is. This means what is included and excluded. Exclusions could be on the basis of geography, e.g. UK sites only, or on the basis of services, where a particular practice area is not deemed to be included.

Some examples of scope are outlined below. To better illustrate the point some non-legal examples have been included.

- **A major London practice:** The business continuity management system relating to the provision of legal services.
- **A food company:** The business continuity management system relating to the receipt, storage and movement of raw material; quality control (food safety and compliance); manufacture and processing of products from raw materials to finished products.
- **A local authority:** The business continuity management system in relation to the provision of local government, specifically excluding residential care facilities.

> **Note:** Do not exclude a sector or service that is key to your ability to deliver client services. It is impossible to imagine IT being excluded from any firm's business continuity plans.

3.3 Business continuity awareness training

It is useful to have a statement to bring business continuity to prominence in the practice. An example on the topic of training of staff is offered at **Annex 3A**.

3.4 Strategy document

Practices may wish to publish a strategy document that records overarching strategies, the business continuity strategy and supporting departmental policies on the basis of which plans can be developed.

This is the lever that can move the practice to action. It should be signed by the executive group to give it the necessary credibility and power. An example is offered at **Annex 3B** and should be amended appropriately.

This document outlines the overall strategies and supporting policies on which business continuity plans are to be devised.

3.5 Planning assumptions

It is very difficult indeed to generate any plan without at least some assumptions being made. For example, if one plans to drive from London to Edinburgh one assumes, all things being equal, that the car will work and that petrol stations will be open.

The planning assumptions below allow the scale of the response to be determined. For example, the HR department, which might be caring for casualty welfare, assumes that it needs to plan for 20 per cent casualties. Of course there could be more than 20 per cent casualties; if there are then we know we need to divert resources to this area. If there are fewer than 20 per cent casualties, then we know we can cope within the existing plan.

Some draft planning assumptions which fit most business models, as they are based on percentages, are outlined below. They should be reviewed for the context and location of the firm in question.

3.5.1 Planning assumptions inherent

- Up to 20 per cent of the staff, visitor and contractor total on any site at any time could be casualties in an event and some of those casualties might become fatalities, estimated at 5 per cent.
- Any site could be lost (destroyed) totally by a number of causes or the building may not be usable subsequently in the short to medium term.
- Access to the site could be denied for a considerable period of time (up to one month) without the building being destroyed.

- The only conceivable threat to the firm as a whole is either severe pandemic or catastrophic IT failure.

3.6 Overarching strategy and supporting departmental policies

As a quick checklist and self-assessment tool, the matrix at **Annex 3C** may be filled in and developed with the practice.

Annex 3A

Business continuity awareness training statement

[*Practice name*] recognises that a powerful tool in minimising the threats to business continuity is comprehensive training and awareness education. The Management Team supports the ongoing education and training of all relevant employees, and follows three guideline recommendations:

- effective communication planning;
- a change management approach to training; and
- measuring the effectiveness of awareness training.

[*Name of department/team/individual*] reviews the current awareness training programme [*insert frequency*]. The education programme as outlined in [*details of where outlined*] covers specific training, records, reports, metrics and individual notices.

Review of all awareness training and reporting is undertaken [*insert frequency*] by [*name of department/team/individual*], or in response to factors that result in changes to the business, security, threat, vulnerability or risk landscape.

[*Name*] is responsible for the overall delivery of business continuity training and awareness programmes, in liaison with [*other appropriate departments or personnel*] as required.

Extraordinary awareness training for employees may be sanctioned by [*name*], based on findings and recommendations from relevant parties including but not limited to the Management Team, HR, Security or Information Security Manager. Departures from the business continuity awareness training programme are indicated in reports as additional extraordinary items.

Awareness education and training programmes are organised in accordance with the generic template found [*location*], with specific help by [*name*] located [*location*].

Annex 3B
Overarching and supporting strategies and policies

1   Overarching strategies

1.1 *Strategy in normality:* To provide excellent services to our clients.

1.2 *During a disruptive event:* The business continuity strategy is to maintain our client services with minimal interruption thereby maintaining the overarching strategy in normality.

2   Pandemic planning

2.1 The practice recognises the inevitability of a pandemic occurring at some time.

2.2 A comprehensive pandemic annex to the main plan will be maintained.

2.3 It will be based on best practice guidance and the most up-to-date advice on infection rates and mortality as published by:

- the UK Health Protection Agency;
- the UK Department of Health;
- the World Health Organization.

3   Methodology

3.1 The practice has adopted the UK's 'Gold (strategic level), Silver (tactical level), and Bronze (operational response level)' system (as recommended in current Home Office advice literature) as a model on which to base its own management response to serious incidents. The system as applied to the firm is outlined below.

4   Gold: Strategic Control Group (SCG)

4.1 The SCG comprises: [*sample list:*

- Managing Partner/Head of Legal
- Chief Operating Officer
- Finance Director
- Head of HR
- Head of Facilities Management
- All department/team heads]

4.2 The role of the SCG is to determine strategy in an incident and to prioritise issues affecting the firm as a whole and give directions to 'Silver teams' at office locations for action. The SCG will also deal with any press or media inquiries.

5   Silver: Incident Management Team (IMT)

5.1 The IMT comprises: [*sample list:*

- Local IMT leader
- Heads of legal teams as required
- Local support staff representatives
- Secretarial support team]

5.2 The role of the IMT is to:

- apply strategic direction in the local context;
- issue local direction and tasking to operational response groups;
- report progress and issues to the SCG.

6   Bronze: Operational Response Teams (ORTs)

6.1 The composition of ORTs will vary depending on the nature of the incident. ORTs will work to the direction of the local IMT leader.

7   Strategic priorities in order

7.1 No plan can anticipate all eventualities. Therefore this outline prioritisation of responses and accompanying strategies serves as guide for anyone involved in an incident response.

7.2 They are:

- The safety and well-being of people, including contractors and visitors.
- [*Insert any other priorities*].

7.3 The priorities are illustrated diagrammatically below:

[*Insert your own diagram*]

8   Management systems

8.1 The practice's incident management system is outlined diagrammatically below (**Figure 3.1**).

9   Media team

9.1 The Media team's supporting strategy to the overarching crisis strategy is to:

- maintain our reputation by being [*insert details of media strategy*].

9.2 Therefore in order that the practice recovers from an incident with the clients' confidence, we have to conduct a successful media policy. To this end, we will:

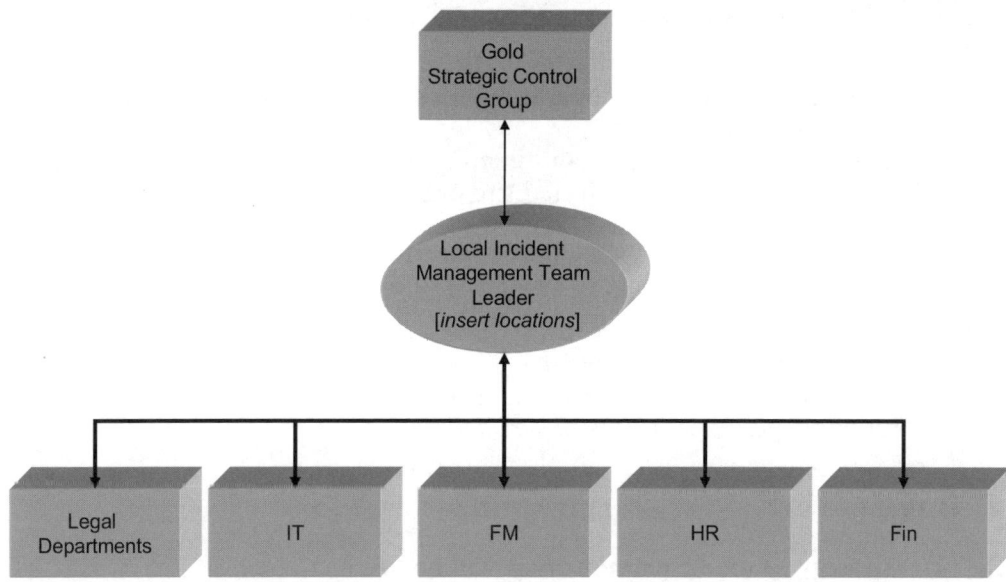

Figure 3B.1 Example business continuity management structure

- have in place an effective crisis communications strategy;
- have employees assigned tasks and roles which will allow them to deal successfully and skilfully with a crisis.

10 HR team

10.1 The HR team's supporting strategy to the overarching crisis strategy is to:

- provide appropriate support and [*insert details of HR strategy*].

10.2 Therefore, in order that the firm recovers from an incident with an enhanced reputation, we need to ensure that all elements of staff, contractors' and visitors' needs during and post-incident are catered for to an appropriate level. To this end, we will:

- maintain up-to-date staff and contractor lists;
- liaise with security through Facilities Management to obtain visitor lists at the time of an incident.

11 Facilities Management department

11.1 The Facilities Management department's strategy will be to:

- ensure that at all times adequate premises are available to the firm to provide [*insert details*].

11.2 To achieve this strategy the anticipated incident can be viewed in three stages:

- The initial occupation and operation of alternative mutual aid or commercial disaster recovery (DR) sites.
- The recovery of documents and items from the affected site.
- The reoccupation of the affected site or the procurement of new premises.

11.3 Therefore the Facilities Management department will ensure the following are maintained at a state of readiness to be deployed or invoked quickly:

- Document and buildings recovery [*insert details*].
- Insurance policies [*insert details*].
- DR sites and mutual aid [*insert details*].
- Alternative permanent sites [*insert details*].

12   IT team

12.1 The strategy of the IT team in crisis will be to:

- recover the IT systems in a progressive fashion according to the [*insert details*].

12.2 Therefore the IT team will, in addition to 'normal IT policies', ensure that [*insert details*].

13   Finance team

13.1 The Finance team's supporting strategy to the overarching crisis strategy is to ensure the financial stability of the firm during and following any incident.

13.2 Therefore the Finance team will [*insert details*].

14   Maintenance of the plans and rehearsals and miscellaneous doctrines

14.1 This section is applicable to all the office locations.

14.2   *Reviews of risk:*

- Reviews of risk will be undertaken by [*names*] at site level.
- Sources to be consulted include:
  - local risk registers;
  - local resilience forums in the UK;
  - police and emergency services.

14.3 *Rolling business impact analysis (BIA):* A BIA will be conducted on all new significant IT systems, applications and business developments (e.g. acquisition of another firm, expansion into another country) and the results incorporated into the firm's BIA. Appropriate resilience will then be applied.

14.4 *Training and exercising:* The practice undertakes to train staff appropriately.

14.5 *Alternatives and deputies:* The practice will identify an alternative or deputy for all roles and posts in the business continuity plan.

Annex 3C

Strategy matrix

Overarching strategy in normality	
Overarching business continuity strategy	
Supporting policies for departments/teams	
HR	
Media	
Finance	
IT	
Facilities Management	
Others	
Comments and notes to self:	

4 Understanding the practice

Note: Requirement 2.3(a) of the Lexcel standard requires firms to evaluate their potential risks and the likelihood of their impact. Understanding the practice has to be seen in the context of business continuity and the two main methodologies for achieving this are the business impact analysis and the risk assessment.

There is an active debate as to which one should be done first. To some extent their relationship is symbiotic and therefore it does not really matter.

The risk assessment will help practices identify what the threats are to the firm. The business impact analysis is a measure of how much can be lost and how fast. This understanding then drives anticipated recovery times and informs a lot of the planning that is necessary. In this instance we will deal with the risk assessment first.

4.1 Risk assessment

Imagine the practice and its location interacting with its clients and the community. The threats can be external or internal, natural or technological and combinations thereof. The following section is a comprehensive methodology for undertaking a risk assessment for the firm. Naturally it has to be tailored to the individual organisation.

4.1.1 Purpose

The purpose of this section is to provide a methodology for the practice's personnel to follow and apply when undertaking a site risk assessment in order to complete a site risk register.

The aim of the site risk assessment process is to understand and evaluate the risks/threats to the site, its critical activities and the resources which directly support the site critical activities (people, premises, ICT, assets and third-party providers/suppliers). This should enable the practice to maintain existing risk controls and, where deemed necessary, practical and proportionate, to implement additional site risk controls in order to:

- reduce the likelihood of a disruption;
- shorten the period of a disruption if the risk occurs;
- limit the impact of a disruption if the risk occurs.

It is important to understand from the outset that a risk assessment is a subjective process as, by definition, risk is an abstraction which has not yet occurred.

4.1.2 Scope

There are many risk categories including strategic, programme, project, change management, financial and operational risk, for example. The site risk register scope comprises operational risks only, which are 'the risks or threats to day-to-day operations' (BS 31100). Other risk categories are out of scope at the site assessment level but could be included in the strategic risk register as part of the practice's wider risk management framework.

The risks in scope are those which threaten:

- the site/premises;
- the site critical functions and activities (day-to-day operations);
- the resources that directly support and enable the site critical activities and functions (people, premises, ICT, assets/equipment and third-party providers/suppliers).

4.2 Overview and use

The site risk assessment methodology should be referred to throughout the completion of the site risk register document. The methodology comprises five phases:

Phase	Description
1	Identify the risks and identify the likely effect(s) of each risk if it should occur
2	Establish the existing risk controls in situ
3	Assess the risks based on the risk controls in situ: • assess the likelihood of the risk occurring • assess the impact if the risk occurs • establish the risk rating
4	Select the risk strategy for each risk (treat, tolerate, transfer or terminate) and have senior management review the risk strategies
5	Identify additional practical and proportionate risk controls which: • should be implemented for 'treat' risks • could be implemented for other risk strategies

Each phase is explained below. Within each phase, reference is made to the completion of the relevant column(s) of the site risk register at **4.4**.

4.2.1   Phase 1: Identify the site risks and the effect(s) of each risk should it occur

To assist in both identifying risks and understanding the effect(s) of each risk should it occur, the site risk leader should gather a small site management team comprising function or department heads or site subject heads as appropriate and proportionate. A workshop should be conducted with this team to identify site risks in the following four categories:

- Physical
- Human
- External
- Technical

Physical risks are those risks which relate to the location of the practice and its buildings. The practice, even if in a multi-occupancy building, should have some influence over the risks and can plan to mitigate the effect of the risk, should it occur, e.g. a fire in site premises or a flood of the basement.

Human risks are more subjective in nature and are difficult in some cases to forecast, but the practice can plan to mitigate the effect of these risks, e.g. increased IT security if downsizing, or reviews of terms and conditions if staff turnover rises.

External risks relate to issues normally beyond the control of the practice but which can nonetheless be anticipated and planned for. Examples include strikes, demonstrations, adverse weather, etc. Also note any neighbouring business that might create risks to your own site, e.g. political party buildings, industrial or construction sites, and any potential focus of demonstrations.

Technical risks are those related to the IT and communications systems of the practice. Often these are closely linked, e.g. phones using the Internet (VOIP), contracted out IT provision, telephone company resilience, etc. Often regulatory and compliance risks focus on these areas, e.g. data protection, financial regulations, etc.

It is often difficult to be prescriptive about the area into which the risk is categorised, as they are often linked. By way of illustration, a disgruntled member of staff might download personal data to his or her own home PC. This is a human act with technical and regulatory repercussions which could anger clients, leading to a loss of reputation and thus business. What is important is not exactly where on the diagram the risk is placed, rather that it is identified and subsequently managed.

External information sources should also be referenced to assist in identifying risks. Sources of risk information include:

- Map study of local area and local knowledge
- Internal audit, performance, IT security reports and assessments
- Community risk registers and other associated local authority reports
- Environment Agency flood maps

Figure 4.1 provides a starting point risk/threat map at site level.

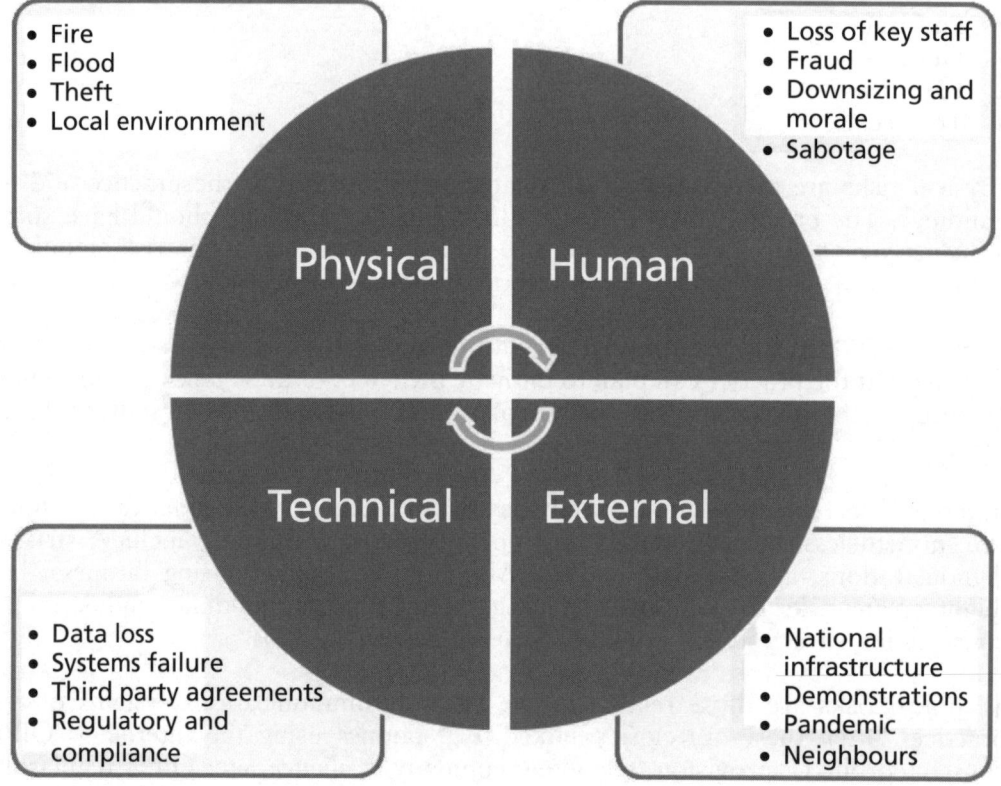

Figure 4.1 Risk/threat map starting point

4.2.2   Phase 2: Establish the existing risk controls in situ

It is important that the risk assessment is made with due consideration for the existing control measures in situ. A 'risk control' is any system, process or procedure that mitigates a risk by:

- reducing the likelihood of a disruption;
- shortening the period of a disruption if it occurs;
- limiting the impact of a disruption if it occurs.

Using the risk of fire at a site as an example, controls in situ may include fire detection and suppression systems, a regularly rehearsed fire evacuation procedure, a validated contingency plan to conduct critical activities from different sites and so on. Controls in situ should be noted in column (d) of the site risk register.

4.2.3 Phase 3: Assessment of the risks

In order to subjectively assess each risk or threat, the 'likelihood' of each risk/threat occurring and the consequent 'impact' should be assessed using the matrix in **Figure 4.2** and the definitions below.

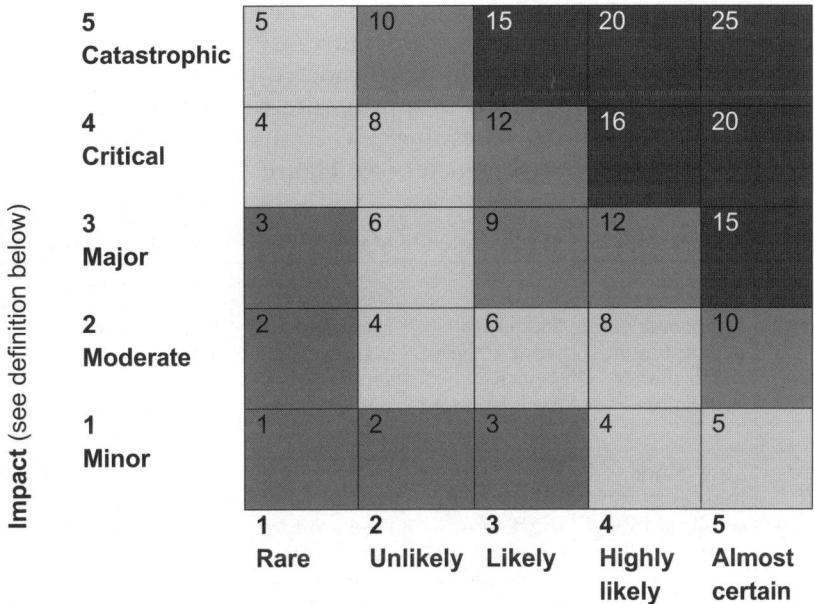

Figure 4.2 Likelihood and impact matrix

Likelihood definitions

The likelihood of a risk occurring comprises both the anticipated probability and frequency of the risk occurring as below. The subjective assessment of likelihood should factor both elements and the rating (1 to 5) should be noted in column (e) of the site risk register.

Rating	Term	Probability of occurrence	Frequency of occurrence
1	Rare	Below 10%	May occur in the next 25–50 years
2	Unlikely	11–35%	May occur in the next 10–25 years
3	Likely	36–65%	May occur in the next 5–10 years
4	Highly likely	66–90%	May occur in the next 1–5 years
5	Almost certain	Above 90%	May occur in the next year

Impact definitions

The subjective assessment of the impact of a risk when it occurs should be made in consideration of the impact definitions at **Figure 4.3**. The 'Work activity/service performance disruption' impact should be considered for all risks. The other types of impact should only be considered if appropriate to each risk and if helpful in contributing to subjective impact assessment. The impact rating (1 to 5) should be noted in column (f) of the site risk register (see **Figure 4.4**).

Impact rating	Minor	Moderate	Major	Critical	Catastrophic
Type of impact	1	2	3	4	5
Work activity/ service performance disruption	Minor work activity/ service performance disruption	Moderate work activity/ service performance disruption	Major work activity/ service performance disruption	Critical work activity/ service performance disruption	Catastrophic work activity/ service performance disruption
Staff health/ loss of staff capacity	Very minor injuries to staff or minor loss of staff capacity	Minor injuries to staff with short-term health effects or moderate loss of staff capacity	Major injuries to staff with medium-term health effects or major loss of staff capacity	A staff fatality and/ or multiple major injuries with permanent health effects or critical loss of staff capacity	Multiple staff fatalities and/ or multiple major injuries with permanent health effects or catastrophic loss of staff capacity
Reputational loss	Adverse mention in local press/ media, legal community, local publications	Significant negative coverage in local press/ media, legal community, local or trade publications	Significant negative coverage in regional press/ media, legal community, local or regional publications	Limited negative coverage in national press/media	Significant negative coverage in national press/media

Impact rating	Minor	Moderate	Major	Critical	Catastrophic
Type of impact	1	2	3	4	5
Regulatory/ compliance breach	Informal questions from the SRA or other regulatory body (HSE)	Formal questions from the SRA or other regulatory body (HSE)	Significant investigation by the SRA or other regulatory body (HSE)	Formal inquiry by the SRA or other regulatory body (HSE)	Prosecution for regulatory/ compliance failures
Financial loss/ cost	Loss/cost of up to £10,000	Loss/cost of £10,000 to £100,000	Loss/cost of £100,000 to £500,000	Loss/cost of £500,000 to £1 million	Loss/cost of more than £1 million
Information/ data loss	Loss of unrestricted information	Small and contained loss of restricted information	Large and uncontained loss of restricted information	Loss of strategic confidential information	Loss of strategic secret information
ICT service loss	Short-term loss of single service	Long-term loss of single service	Short-term loss of multiple services	Long-term loss of multiple services	Long-term loss of all services
Premises loss	Light/ superficial damage. Can be responded to within normal arrangements. No access or movement restrictions	Moderate damage within limited area of one building. Temporary loss of limited internal space	Major damage to one or more site buildings. Specialist contractors needed for repair/ recovery. Short-term denial of access	Significant damage to site buildings. Specialist contractors needed for repair/ recovery. Mid-term denial of access	Total loss of one or more site buildings requiring long-term working at alternative sites

Figure 4.3 Impact definitions

The final step of this phase is to establish the risk rating which is the total of multiplying the likelihood rating (column (e)) and the impact rating (column (f)). The risk rating should be noted in column (g) and the colour of the risk rating box should be filled and match the risk rating colour detailed in **Figure 4.2** above.

4.2.4 Phase 4: Select the risk strategy for each risk

The risk ratings should broadly be interpreted as below:

Risk rating	Risk rating considerations/action
Very high	These are very high risks for the site which require urgent management attention and action. Where practical and proportionate to do so, new risk controls must be implemented as soon as possible to reduce the risk rating. New controls should aim to: • reduce the likelihood of a disruption; • shorten the period of a disruption if it occurs; • limit the impact of a disruption if it occurs. These risks should be monitored by senior management on a regular basis.
High	These are high risks which require management attention and action. Where practical and proportionate to do so, new risk controls should be implemented to reduce the risk rating. These risks should be monitored by senior management on a regular basis.
Moderate	These are moderate risks. New risk controls should be considered and scoped. Where practical and proportionate, selected controls should be prioritised for implementation. These risks require regular management monitoring.
Low	These risks are unlikely to occur and are not significant in their impact. They can be managed within the existing operational framework and require minimal monitoring.

The site risk assessment team should then consider and establish the appropriate risk strategies for each risk given the risk rating considerations above. There are four options:

Risk strategy (solution)	Description
Treat	Implement and monitor the effectiveness of new controls to reduce the risk rating. This may involve significant resources to achieve (IT infrastructure for data replication/storage, cross-training of specialist staff, providing standby premises, etc.) or may comprise a number of low cost, or cost-neutral, mitigating measures which cumulatively reduce the risk rating (a validated business continuity plan, documented and regularly rehearsed building evacuation procedures, etc.).
Tolerate	A risk may be acceptable without any further action being taken depending on the risk appetite of the organisation. Also, while there may clearly be additional new controls which could be implemented to 'treat' a risk, if the cost of treating the risk is greater than the anticipated impact and loss should the risk occur, then it may be decided to tolerate the risk and maintain existing risk controls only.
Transfer	It may be possible to transfer the risk to a third party (conventional insurance or service provision (outsourcing or off-shoring)). However, it is not possible to transfer the responsibility for the risk; this remains with the firm.
Terminate	In some circumstances it may be appropriate or possible to terminate or remove the risk altogether by changing policy, process, procedure or function.

Once the risk strategy has been provisionally selected for each risk and noted in column (h) of the site risk register, the site risk leader and the senior management should review and approve the site risk strategies prior to implementation.

4.2.5 Phase 5: Identify new risk controls

As stated above, 'risk control' is any system, process or procedure that mitigates the risk by:

- reducing the likelihood of a disruption;
- shortening the period of a disruption if it occurs;
- limiting the impact of a disruption if it occurs.

Typically, many of the new risk controls are identified during 'Phase 2: Establish the existing risk controls in situ'. However, consideration should be given to all possible, practical and proportionate new risk controls for each individual risk at this stage.

Some new controls may:

- require significant resources for infrastructure, systems, equipment or training;
- be close to cost-neutral, requiring procedural change or some limited staff awareness or cross-training;
- apply to many of the risks in the site register; others will apply to a single risk only;
- build on existing controls. For example, an existing control may be an out-dated business continuity plan and so the new control may be to revise and update the business continuity plan, to train the necessary staff in the plan and validate the plan and the staff training with an annual exercise.

New risk controls for consideration should be noted in column (i) of the site risk register and be approved by the firm's management prior to implementation. Note that in the interest of continuous improvement, the cost-neutral, procedural and process-based new controls should be implemented for a risk even if the risk strategy is not to 'treat' the risk.

4.3 Review of site risk register

Once completed this risk register should be reviewed on an annual basis as directed on the cover sheet by the site risk leader and by senior management. It may be reviewed sooner in the event of significant organisational or site change.

4.4 The firm's risk assessment point of contact

Practices need to decide the appropriate person to whom any questions regarding this site risk register methodology or the site risk register template should be directed.

A completed risk register might look as in **Figure 4.4**.

Risk no.	Risk identified	Likely effect if risk occurs	Risk controls in situ	Likelihood of risk occurring	Impact if risk occurs	Risk rating	Risk strategy	Potential new risk controls	Risk owner	Remarks
(a)	(b)	(c)	(d)	(e)	(f)	(g)	(h)	(i)	(j)	(k)
Technical/economic – internal risks										
R001	IT failure, Carpe Diem, time keeping	Reversion to manual time keeping Loss of accounts as it is linked to Elite to generate invoicing and reconciliation Backlog of work on manual inputting for finance department Only sustainable for 5 days	None	3	3	9	TREAT	Mirrored system failover would reduce effect to practically nil Anticipated in 2015 review annually	James Brown Mary Green	Check this on BIA interviews

Figure 4.4 Completed risk register

4.5 The business impact analysis

The business impact analysis (BIA) is probably the most time consuming part of the whole process of evaluating risk and depends largely on face-to-face interviews. If one merely holds awareness sessions and then ask departments to 'fill it in themselves' the result is usually inaccurate.

The BIA examines the effects of the loss of an IT application or a business process that depends upon it and therefore the effect that it would have on any firm.

If we refer back to the risk assessment in the risk register above, the loss of Carpe Diem (the time management system) would not seriously threaten most firms but its impact might be greater if the loss occurred at financial year end as invoices could not be generated and final accounts would be impossible.

Note that increasingly often applications are linked to others so in many cases the loss of a simple application can lead to the loss of a business process. Therefore, always predicate the effect of a loss of an application, or thereby a business process, as occurring at the least convenient time.

Using the example of **Figure 4.5** can help you to compile what is required to maintain critical activities of the practice. This is most easily done by department.

4.6 Key products and services

These are what define the firm as being a law firm. In the example given at **Figure 4.5** a law firm ceases to have the 'quality of being lawyers' if it cannot manage the transfer of funds. An incident does not really matter too much if at the time of that incident background conveyancing work can continue. If something is a contractual obligation it matters greatly if this cannot be provided. The BIA reflects the balance of key products and services that practices offer. This has to be decided by you for your firm.

4.7 Critical activities

The next stage is to decide what critical activities one or more of the key services depend upon, for example conveyancing is impossible to arrange without access to banking services. Another example in a legal environment is that it might be impossible to conduct client meetings without premises as the nature of the business needs face-to-face meetings.

4.8 Resources and assets

Finally, identify what it is in terms of resources and assets that supports the critical activity that renders the key product and services. In **Figure 4.5** below it is quite evident that the IT system (a resource or asset) that runs the transfer of funds (a critical activity) determines the ability to provide conveyancing (a key product and service).

Although there is a wide range of differences between practices, examples for legal work may include a resource or asset being the ability to record time worked on client matters on an IT-based application. The critical activity is the billing of the client for work done, the key product and service for the finance department being to bring in money owed.

The whole process is outlined in **Figure 4.5**:

1	2	3	4	5
Identify key services	**Determine critical activities**	**List resources and assets**	**Calculate business impact of failure**	**Specify timescales and restore points**
• Conveyancing • Mergers and Acquisitions	• Receipt of information • Process documentation • Transfer of funds • Client meetings	• Staff • Work sites • Facilities • IT/Internet • Databases • Information • Third party support	• Loss of applications system • Absence of business process	• MTPD • RTO • RPO

Figure 4.5 Identifying resources and assets supporting delivery of key products and services

- Maximum tolerable period of disruption (MTPD) – durations after which an organisation's viability will be irrevocably threatened if the product or service delivery cannot be resumed.
- Business recovery time objective (RTO) – target time for the resumption of product, service or activity after an incident.
- Recovery point objective (RPO) – the point in time to which data have to be recovered in order to resume ICT services.

Then it is time to score the business impact. Practices need to determine the impact of the loss of the applications system or business process for each period of time, defined as follows:

Score	Impact	Definition
1	Inconvenient	A minor irritant which can be worked around almost indefinitely but is nonetheless distracting, e.g. heating failure malfunction in meeting rooms, in summer
2	Troublesome	A minor irritant that needs to be fixed in the near future, e.g. time keeping system failure – people can revert to manual or work around
3	Awkward	Something which actually prevents some form of work being done, e.g. access to electronic case management systems. Although it can be done in another way or fashion, this cannot be sustained for long
4	Very difficult	Something with an immediate adverse effect that will have wider and serious ramifications very quickly unless remedied shortly, e.g. loss of water supply to the building
5	Catastrophic	Immediate adverse effects needing immediate remedial action at the cost of any other actions, e.g. loss of power to the building

Note this might be in regard to the following classes of effects of the loss of system or process:

- Disruption to work
- Financial loss
- Client impact
- Damage to reputation
- Regulatory, compliance and legal issues

This information then needs to be placed in a matrix for later reference; an example is offered at **Annex 4A**.

Note:

- The timeframe is arbitrary and needs to be set by the firm.
- All 'time' runs from the point of the incident occurring not the point from which it is noticed or diagnosed.
- In the worked example at **Annex 4A** the issue becomes critical at day 2 and therefore has to be recovered sooner.
- Basically the critical line in the example is the score of 4 in the client impact at day 2 of an outage. It does not really matter that there are worse scores this. It is this point that determines the RTO and RPO.

Now you have to determine in more detail the solution for people, premises, technology and suppliers.

The practice should then estimate the minimum resources that each activity will require on resumption. These could include:

- staff resources, including numbers, skills and knowledge (people);
- the work site and facilities required (premises);
- supporting technology, plant and equipment (technology);
- provision of information to enable work to continue (information); and
- external services and suppliers (suppliers).

See **Annex 4B**.

4.9 The dispersal matrix: who goes where and when?

Having identified the criticality of various issues you can record and summarise this and the results of the matrix above on a BIA sheet.

This sheet should also include the information as to where the staff will be located for ongoing work, which is often referred to as a 'dispersal matrix'.

An example is offered at **Annex 4C**.

Annex 4A

Risk matrix

Duration of loss/ timeframe	Disruption to work	Financial loss	Client impact	Damage to reputation	Regulatory, compliance and legal issues	Maximum tolerable period of disruption (MTPD)			Recovery time objective (RTO)	Recovery point objective (RPO)
						Max time from the start of the incident that the activity has to be resumed	Minimum level of activity on resumption of service as a % of functionality	Length of time to recover activity to 100%	Has to be less than the MTPD	When is the data recovered back to in time? Nil would be without losing any data
Loss of the database for [*insert department*]										
1 hour	1		1							
2 hours	1	1	1							
4 hours	1	1	1	1						
8 hours/ 1 day	1	1	1	1	1	[7:59]	[50%]	[8 hours]	[4 hours]	[2 hours]
2 days	3	2	4	2	1					
4 days	4	3	4	3	2					
One week/ 7 days	5	3	5	4	2					
Two weeks	5	4	5	4	3					
One month	5	5	5	5	5					

Annex 4B

Minimum resources

No.	Dept	People	Premises	Technology	Suppliers
1					
2					
3					
4					
5					
6					
Comments and notes to self:					

Annex 4C
Dispersal matrix

No.	Unit location numbers	Critical numbers to function	Critical equipment/ systems and apps	MTPD RTO RPO	Critical information/ locations	Inter-dependency and clients	DR site and time to reach it	Home working	Other
1	Real estate [*insert location*]	(24)	Laptops with [MS Office Documentum MP5]	4 hours 2 hours nil	Deeds Land Registry website Crown Court	Corporate Law [*insert location*] RBS HSBC	[*Insert location*] DR site 2 hours (12)	(12)	(26)
2									

5 The planning process

Now that you know what and whom you need, where, why and when, you need the structure of how to deliver it.

5.1 The structure

Before your firm can plan anything you need first to determine the structure of the response and how it will be managed. Ideally there should be little difference between normal and incident management structures. This will reduce any need to take into account any new management methods in an incident.

Your task is to design the idealised business continuity incident management structure for the firm. Points to note:

- Ideally it should be based on the 'Gold (strategic), Silver (tactical), Bronze (operational)' system, which is the government and emergency services method.
- The size of the practice and the existing management structure (which will be altered as little as possible) might preclude a three-tier system. In this case the two tiers to merge would be Gold and Silver with the managing partner or Head of Legal being in effect the Silver commander.
- The span of command should ideally be no more than five members of staff because with more than five people reporting to a person in an incident they tend to become overburdened.
- The chain of command should also be no more than three deep. If this is exceeded then there is increasing difficulty in passing information between layers of management.
- Other possible combinations and techniques are available and some brief structures are outlined below.
- The main difficulty a lot of firms experience is the 'flat hierarchy' syndrome.
- Other issues concern the need for consultation in a partnership. The way around this is to agree that in the event of an incident, a few of the senior partners can take decisions on behalf of the firm without recourse to a protracted meeting.

5.2 The plan

The plan will vary tremendously between organisations. In essence keep it as simple as possible and only include detail that informs someone of what to do.

To avoid it becoming very long and needing reissuing to all concerned even for minor changes, it is suggested that each department has its own discrete plan and that all plans are 'sectionalised' so that reissues are not administratively burdensome.

Outlined below is a template that can be adapted for any department or unit ranging from the strategic group to facilities management or HR. In this case it is for the Silver (tactical) level leader.

In the example one or two worked tasks and instructions have been included so as to illustrate the level of detail potentially required.

Annex 5A
Business continuity plan

[*Name of firm*]

Crisis Management Team leader: [*Name*]

Deputy: [*Name*]

Location: [*location*]

Date: [*date*]

Issue: [*version*]

Important: This document contains staff contact information and should be used for business continuity purposes only. It is the personal responsibility of all plan holders to secure their respective copies to ensure the confidentiality of the information within.

Table of contents

Annex	Content/title	Applicable to	Page
	CMT contact list	All	
		All	
	Telephone cascade system	All	
		All	
		All	
	Log sheet	All	
		HR	
		PR	
		PR	
		FM & IT	
		FM & IT	
		FM	
		FM	

SECTION 1: Introduction

Version control and review

The internal and external contacts directory at [*practice name*] is to be reviewed on a [*insert details, e.g. quarterly basis*]; the remainder of this document is to be reviewed annually or as may be required in the light of changing business circumstances and events.

Document history

Version no.	Date	Authors	Description of change
1.0			New plan
2.0			Full review – new plan

Distribution/storage

Action: 2 copies: hard copy (office); soft copy on USB (home)	Information
All CMT members	CMT Battle Box (x 3)

SECTION 2: Business continuity plan

Business continuity policy essentials

All Crisis Management Team (CMT) members must be familiar with the practice's business continuity policy essentials set out below. Plan users should refer to this page during an incident.

Purpose

To provide our clients with the highest service levels of any law firm.

Business continuity strategy

[To minimise the interruption to normal levels of operational functionality and service to all the firm's stakeholders, operational partners and staff.]

or

[To maintain our client services with minimal interruption so as to continue to provide the highest service levels of any law firm.]

Scope

The scope of [*name of firm*] business continuity management system includes [*specify departments*] and all the firm's staff.

It also includes embedded contractors and partners who may be critical to its recovery.

Strategic recovery objectives

- To ensure the safety and welfare of the firm's staff, contractors, visitors and the public.
- To restore facilities at affected site(s) [*insert location(s)*].
- To restore IT at affected site(s).

- To resume fee-earning operations as quickly as possible.
- To provide services and facilities to operational partners and stakeholders.

These strategic recovery objectives are supported by department-level business continuity strategies within the Facilities, Media, IT, HR, Company Finance and Business Continuity CMT.

Planning assumptions

- A threat or an incident could be internal or external and could affect the sites at [*insert locations*] or impact on an area-wide scale (local, regional or national).
- A site could be lost (destroyed) totally by any of a number of causes.
- Access could be denied to a site for up to [*x*] months; one or both sites may suffer from the same event and be similarly affected.
- [*x*]% of people in the firm's premises could be casualties and [*x*]% of these casualties could become fatalities. 'People' includes staff, contractors, visitors and the public.
- Significant disruption to IT may occur.
- The only conceivable threat to the firm as a whole is either a severe pandemic or a catastrophic IT failure.

Pandemic planning

- The firm recognises the inevitability of a pandemic occurring at some time.
- A comprehensive pandemic annex to the main plan will be maintained.
- It will be based on best practice guidance and the most up-to-date advice on infection rates and mortality as published by the UK Health Protection Agency, the UK Department of Health and the World Health Organization.

Methodology

The firm has adopted the UK's 'Gold (strategic level), Silver (tactical level) and Bronze (operational response level)' system (as recommended in current Home Office advice literature) as a model on which to base management response to serious incidents. The system as applied to the firm is outlined below:

Gold Strategic Control Group (SCG) comprises:

Name	Appointment	Crisis role

Role

- To determine strategy in an incident.
- To prioritise issues affecting the firm as a whole.
- To give directions to 'Silver teams' at office locations for action.
- To deal with any press or media inquiries.

Silver Incident Management Team (IMT) comprises:

Name	Appointment	Crisis role

Role

- To apply strategic direction in the local context.
- To issue local direction and tasking to operational response groups.
- To report progress and issues to the SCG.

Note: Two IMTs could be active in the case of mutual support requirements being invoked between [specify] and [specify]. The IMT at the unaffected site will probably not be in permanent session and will be acting in support of the affected site.

Bronze Operational Response Teams (ORTs)

The composition of ORTs will vary depending on the nature of the incident. ORTs will work to the direction of their representative in the Silver IMT. Some ORTs may also report back on progress to the SCG, e.g. IT ORTs, but will always take local instruction.

Business continuity responsibilities

- [*Name*], [*job title*], is the Management Board sponsor for business continuity.
- [*Name*], [*job title*], is responsible for the implementation, operation and maintenance of business continuity.
- Every member of staff should be aware of the firm's business continuity policy and have a good understanding of their department's business continuity plan.

Crisis management structure

The firm's crisis management structure (below) is to operate in event of a major incident:

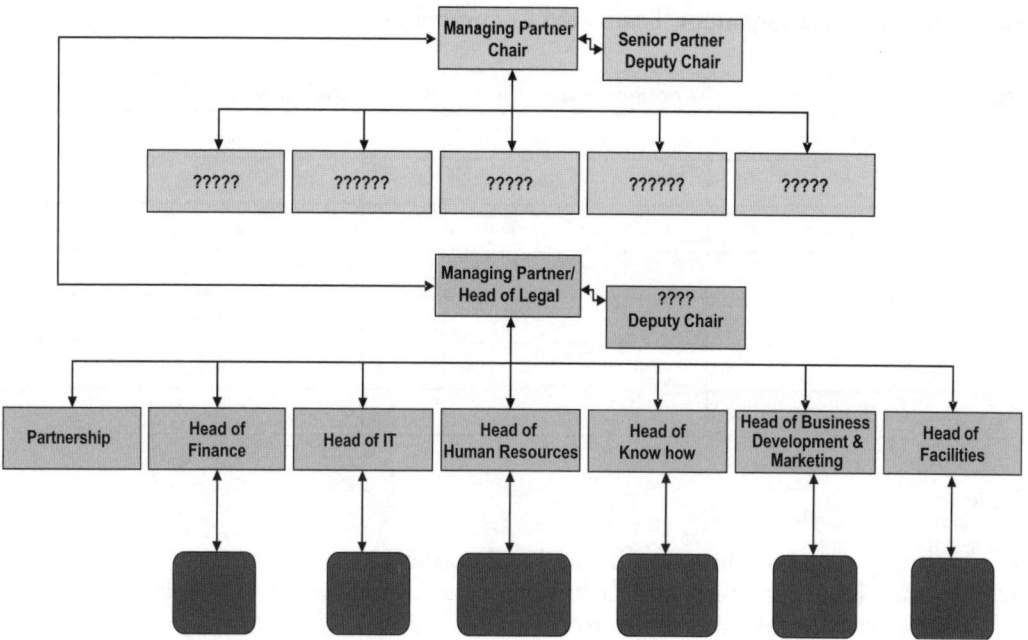

Figure 5.1 Crisis management structure of the firm

Crisis Management Team: roles and responsibilities

Name	Role	CMT function	Responsibilities

Section 3: Crisis Management Team leader

Overview of team plan

Purpose

The purpose of the CMT leader at the firm is to lead and manage response to an incident that seriously interferes with the operational functionality and service. This will minimise disruption and enable the practice to resume normal levels of service and business activity as quickly and as smoothly as possible.

Phases/milestones

The business continuity plan (BCP) is to be delivered in four phases with key milestones monitored and reported up through the chain of command (department to CMT to Managing Partner/Head of Legal):

Phase	Milestones
Phase 1: Incident response	Building confirmed clear of all staff and visitors Invocation decision Staff instructed to move
Phase 2: Action at recovery site	IT systems functional Status report on affected site
Phase 3: Action at BAU site	
Phase 4: Post-incident follow-up	

Phases are illustrated in the plans as follows:

Incident response	Action at recovery site	Recover to BAU site	Post-incident follow-up

Invocation of BCP

- **Authority:** [*e.g.* Managing Partner/Head of Legal]
- **Method:** Initiated by CMT Chair or, in his absence, CMT Deputy Chair by a directive communicated by means of [telephone calls] cascaded to and then down through departments and teams.
- **Telephone/cascade:** Initiated by CMT Chair or Deputy Chair; cascade is at [*insert details*].

Supporting strategies for reference

Media team

The practice's Media team supporting strategy to the overarching crisis strategy is to:

- maintain the reputation of [*practice name*] by [*insert brief details*].

HR team

The firm's HR team supporting strategy to the overarching crisis strategy is to:

- provide appropriate support and assistance to [*insert brief details*].

Facilities Management department

The firm's Facilities Management department supporting strategy to the overarching crisis strategy is to:

- make available to staff, at all times, adequate premises and business infrastructure as to: [*insert brief details*]
  - document and buildings recovery;
  - insurance policies;
  - disaster recovery (DR) sites and mutual aid.

IT team

The strategy of the IT team in crisis will be to:

* recover the IT systems in a progressive fashion [*insert details*].

Finance team

The firm's Finance team supporting strategy to the overarching crisis strategy is to:

* ensure the financial stability of the firm during and following any incident by [*insert details*]

Critical locations

Primary location

(a) Management Board – emergency management room: [*designate room/venue*].
(b) CMT incident control centre: [*designate CMT room/venue*].

Secondary location

(a) Management Board – emergency management room: [*designate room/venue*].
(b) CMT incident control centre: [*designate room/venue*].

The firm's alternative command and control centre:

[*Insert maps as appropriate*]

PHASE 1
CMT leader incident response

Incident response	Action at recovery site	Recover to BAU site	Post-incident follow-up

Objective

Lead the management of the firm's response to an incident so that the Management Board, groups and departments understand what has happened and respond correctly.

- Target completion time: 2 hours

Tasks

Incident response tasks	Instruction
Target completion time: 2 hours	
Obtain any casualty update	Report any casualties to executive and HR for action
Alert recovery site providers and activate BCP	Tel [*insert number*] and give instructions
	Inform all departmental heads that plan is active
Convene initial meeting and confirm times for move to DR site	
Obtain initial facilities report on site and review any timings	
Additional time: 2 hours	
Initiate update reports for clients	Liaise with Media team and gain approval from managing partner
Consider local press release if required	As above

PHASE 2
CMT leader action at recovery site

Incident response	Action at recovery site	Recover to BAU site	Post-incident follow-up

Objective

Lead the management of the recovery of the practice's normal business activities so as to resume normal services and operations after a disruption and possible dislocation as quickly as possible.

- Target completion time: [*number of hours*]

Tasks

Incident response tasks	Instruction
Target completion time: 2–8 hours	
Review systems capabilities	With IT representative, report status to executive *Note*: what is not operational is most important as it can reduce capability
Make adjustments to accommodation requirements based on matters and their criticality	Inform all legal departments as to outcomes
Confirm all remote access systems are functioning	
Target completion time: 8 hours and onwards	

PHASE 3
Recover to business as usual site

Incident response	Action at recovery site	Recover to BAU site	Post-incident follow-up

Objective

Lead the management of the recovery of all the practice's business activities and staff from temporary recovery sites to original workplaces or medium-/long-term alternative sites so as to resume BAU after a disruption/dislocation.

• Target completion time: [*number of hours*]

Tasks

Tasks	Instruction
Obtain site report from FM and make an appreciation of re-occupancy	
Obtain any amendments to seating and or locations that might be required by staff departmental heads	

PHASE 4
Post-incident follow-up action

Incident response	Action at recovery site	Recover to BAU site	Post-incident follow-up

Objective

Review the cause of the disruption/dislocation, the incident response, occupation and set-up of recovery workplaces, the operation of all fee-earning and support activities and the re-occupation and resumption of functions at the original site. This will help assess performance, learn lessons and ensure that individual staff needs have been and are continuing to be met.

Tasks

Tasks	Instruction
Initiate internal inquiry	Determine inquiry leader, duration terms of reference and report format

Annex 5B
Telephone list

Internal contacts

Name	Role	Telephone numbers			E-mail address	Remarks
		Office	Mobile	Home		
						Management Board
						Management Board
						Management Board
						Management Board
						Management Board
						Management Board
						CMT members and deputies
						CMT members and deputies
						CMT members and deputies
						CMT members and deputies
						CMT members and deputies
						CMT members and deputies
						CMT members and deputies
						CMT members and deputies
						CMT members and deputies
						Groups
						Groups
						Groups
						Groups
						Groups

Name	Role	Telephone numbers			E-mail address	Remarks
		Office	Mobile	Home		
						Facilities
						Facilities
						Facilities
						Facilities
						Facilities
						IT
						IT
						IT
						IT

External contacts

Name	Role	Telephone numbers			E-mail address	Remarks
		Office	Mobile	Home		

Annex 5C
Emergency evacuation procedure

[Insert here as appropriate]

Cascade procedures

[Insert here as appropriate]

Example

Name	Calls	Calls
[Name] Head of Office [location] Tel. [number] Mobile [number]	[Name] COO Tel. [number] Mobile [number]	[Name] [Name] [Name] [Name] [Name]
	[Name] FD Tel. [number] Mobile [number]	[Name] [Name] [Name] [Name]
	[Name] HR Director Tel. [number] Mobile [number]	[Name] [Name] [Name] [Name]
	[Name] Facilities Management Tel. [number]	[Name] [Name] [Name]
[Name] Head of Office [location]	[Name] [Name] [Name] [Name]	[Name] [Name] [Name] [Name]

Annex 5D
Incident form template/log sheet

Note: Never erase any entry, just draw a single line through it. Never shred a log sheet.

Date	Name and role	Time on duty
Time	**Event/action/information**	**Carried out by**

Annex 5E
Facilities at alternative command and control centre

Item	Quantity	Remarks
Boardrooms	2	Dependent on availability
Flip charts, stands and coloured pens	4	4 x sets
Record-keeping stationery equipment: – Log sheets – Message pads	10	10 x sets
Catering and personal refreshment facilities		Available 24 hours daily
Security systems including: – Pass issue and control system – Document security system		Available 24 hours daily
Data communications link and e-mail to the firm recovery site		Likely to be [insert location] if [current location] disrupted/denied
Dedicated CMT firm telephone line/ number	1	
Spare telephone lines/numbers	3	Minimum required: 3
Reproductive equipment: – Fax – Photocopier – Printer	1	Minimum 1 of each
Dedicated PC loaded with all standard practice software and printer	1	Minimum: 1 workstation
[Software name] minimum	1	
Hard and soft copies of all the firm BCPs	1	Held by 1. Head of Facilities to hold 1 x hard copy & 1 x soft copy of both CMT & Facilities BCPs in office & home 2. 1 x hard copy of all BCPS held in Facilities Battle Box 3. 3 x hard copies and 2 x soft copies of Facilities BCP to be held in Facilities Battle Box
CMT support staff (CSS): staff appointed by CMT function leaders	4	CSS required for logging, scribing on 3IA charts, typing and general administrative duties
Business Continuity Planning Coordinator	1	
IT support team	1	Determined by Head of IT
Emergency cordon passes	25	Held by PA to Head of Facilities
Emergency kit packs	10	Include: contents lists, distribution lists and site plans of all the firm's locations

6 Training and exercises

> **Note:** Lexcel requirement 2.3(e) states that practices must have a procedure to test the plan annually.

Now, at long last, you have a plan resulting from the BIA and all the work you have undertaken.

First you need to train the staff in the plan. This can be done in many ways. All of them essentially boil down to a thorough review of the plan as it affects the various departments. This will be new to staff, so maintain enthusiasm.

Figure 6.1 illustrates the process by which personal training in seminars grows into desktop exercises and finally full-scale simulations.

Most companies never fully simulate an event as the simulation itself would be too costly and disruptive to the organisation to be worthwhile.

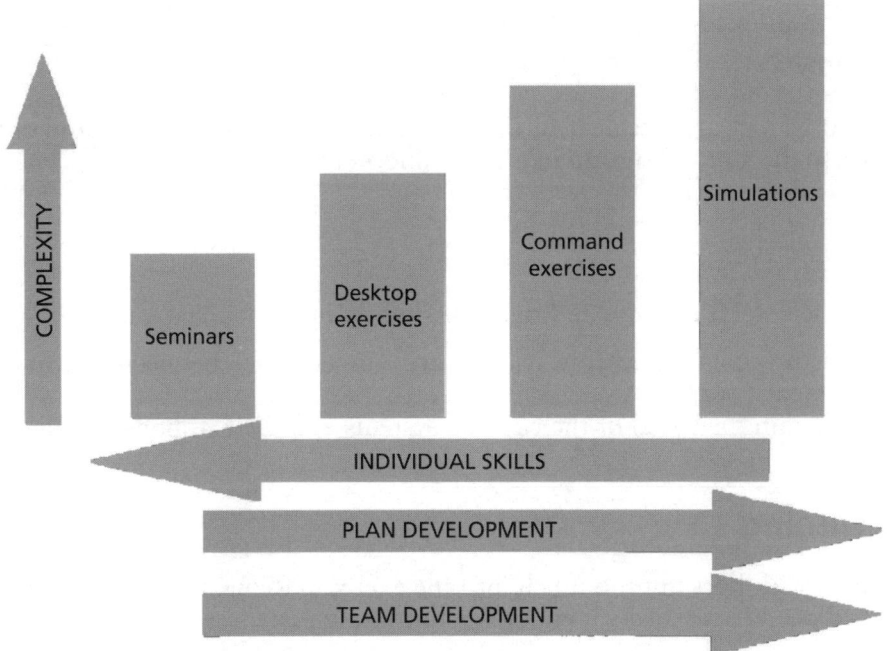

Figure 6.1 Training impact on team

In terms of value for money, regularity of training is more important than scale. For example, four desktop exercises a year may be preferable to two command post exercises or one major simulation.

Exercising a plan is almost a skill in itself and even has its own standards appropriate for its conduct.

Before embarking on any exercise the firm should first determine what it is going to do and why. To do this we tend to use an exercise matrix. It is admittedly formulaic but it works.

6.1 Desktop exercise planning

There are a number of ways of tackling exercises; the most important elements of the process are outlined in **Figure 6.3** to assist you.

Just remember that it is almost impossible to 'test' people, and it puts them off doing such work. So *test* IT systems recovery by all means but *rehearse* or *exercise* the 'people' elements of your plans.

6.2 Aims and objectives

First and foremost clear aims and objectives must be set so that they can be reported back upon later.

6.2.1 Aim

This has to be a clear statement of the overall aim; it should be short and concise, e.g. rehearse the strategic group in a pan London incident.

6.2.2 Objectives

There can be several of these and they are slightly more detailed and specific, e.g.:

1. To ensure communication flows are understood between [individuals/departments, etc.].
2. To ascertain the speed of the cascade systems and their response levels.

6.3 Warning

Most exercise authors put too much into the exercise. Remember that any firm can be stopped dead in its tracks if enough is put into an exercise scenario.

What we are trying to avoid is the exercise scenario with a 'dirty bomb' on a snowy day with IT failure and an outbreak of typhus in the canteen before the structural failure of the building.

To check the logic of your exercise and avoid this temptation we encourage you to fill in the self-assessment tool. A rough example is given at **Annex 6A**. It illustrates the gradation in the exercise between the issues being tackled by an experienced Gold group and an inexperienced Silver team.

Alter the criteria to suit your own firm.

6.4 The master events list

This now brings us to the point where the exercise author has to write the script. It is known as a 'master events list' (MEL). It is worth doing even if the material ends up being delivered on a PowerPoint presentation. The MEL also establishes the success criteria for the exercise based on what the plan says the firm will be doing in such an event. An example is shown at **Annex 6B**.

This can be delivered by live phone feeds or placed on a series of PowerPoint slides in the form of diagrams as illustrated in **Figure 6.2**. Just add them at the time intervals indicated or thereabouts so as to allow participants some time to find the answer.

Incident plus 30 mins 12:55 hrs

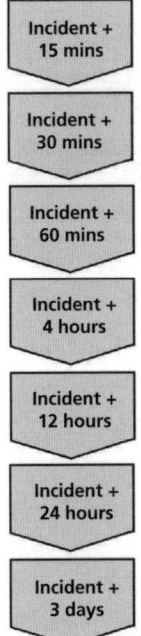

Figure 6.2 Timeline illustrated in desktop exercise

6.4.1 Some general exercise advice

- Allow plenty of time to set up and prepare.
- Technology checks should be done the day before.
- Do a quick run-through of expected events on the morning of the exercise.
- Reiterate introductions, admin and fire drills before the event.
- Provide exercise background (why, how…).
- Begin exercise – enjoy!
- Have a positive closing meeting – it builds confidence.

Time	Considerations/activities	Output
Plan	Why (plans, processes, people)?	Aim
	Key issues to explore?	Objectives
	Who (roles, sites, management level(s))?	Attendance
	Date? Duration? Location?	Date; duration; location
	Scenario options and selection	Scenario
	Structure (immediate response through to recovery phases)?	Structure
	Organisational factors; administration and logistics	Invitations; venue booking
Research	Organisational plans and documents pertinent to the aim and objective	Scenario and structure confirmation and development
	Primary: calls/meeting to build understanding and scenario/master events list (MEL) validity	Source material for situational awareness and scripted events ('injects') in MEL
	Secondary: reports of previous real incidence/exercises; Internet; literature	
Draft MEL	Draft MEL in Word before creating slides (information and expected actions)	Draft MEL containing information and expected actions
	Author the initial situational awareness to build the picture	Initial situational awareness to set the scene
	Each 'inject' should be designed to trigger specific actions detailed in the plans which are being validated in accordance with the exercise aim, objectives and structures	

Time	Considerations/activities	Output
Review	Review the draft MEL with the Exercise Planning Group and any SMEs consulted during the primary research Does the draft MEL meet the aim and objectives for the planned attendees? Do the exercise structure/phases flow? Is the content of the MEL accurate and valid? Are there any sensitivities? Time?	Credible and valid MEL Word doc designed in accordance with the aim, objectives and other key planning criteria
Finalise MEL	Amend and finalise the MEL Word doc Construct the PowerPoint slides. Add maps, media, video clips. Author the opening slides (aim, objective, definitions, etc.) and the closing slides Format any hard copy situational awareness material Author pre-exercise one-page brief	Final MEL Word doc Final PowerPoint presentation exercise slides Pre-exercise one-page brief for all attendees 3 days prior
Rehearse and deliver	**Rehearse:** In room where delivery will occur if possible (IT, seating plan, etc.). Data capture? Determine points/slides to cut if necessary. Time check on delivery? **Deliver:** Speaking order? Ensure plans are validated not regurgitated. Explore the key issues. Make observations. Summarise responses. Time?	Exercise rehearsal Data capture Exercise delivery – aim and objectives achieved
Report	Immediately post-exercise, debrief, capture your observations and understand those captured by whoever was assisting you What will the report be used for? Author the exercise report Initial pages with general exercise detail Annex A: Findings and recommendations against the aims and objectives Annex B: Master events list	Exercise report – lessons identified only

Figure 6.3 Desktop exercise planning aide mémoire (based on 'Desktop exercise planning aide mémoire' © Needhams 1834 Ltd (**www.needhams1834.com**))

6.4.2 Set some rules to ensure that live issues do not get mixed up with the exercise

The following set of rules may be used to brief participants, to ensure as far as possible that there is no 'leakage' from the exercise into reality.

- Information scenarios are to be presented in PowerPoint, etc., followed by time to discuss the decisions that need to be taken and reported back.
- Decisions should be taken where possible in the context of your existing plans.
- Do not have external contact.
- Do not remove any materials relating to the exercise from the room.
- Talk to other people or departments in the room.
- If you require information or updates from external sources, write these down and submit them to the exercise controller, who will respond as appropriate.
- No assumptions. No 'I woulds' – if you are able to do it then do it, but if the infrastructure or practicality of it precludes carrying out the action you cannot 'do' it in the exercise.
- Please ask the exercise controller if anything is not clear or you require further information.
- Go with the intention.

6.4.3 Time keeping and momentum are critical

- Participant discussions will probably take longer than you anticipate.
- Some stages of the scenario will provoke more discussion than others.
- Don't compress lunch/coffee breaks, etc.
- Leave plenty of time for debrief.

6.4.4 Control the pace of the exercise

- Have some questions prepared to stimulate discussions, e.g.:
  - What are the immediate issues?
  - Who are you communicating with?
  - What definitive actions will you take?
  - What are you anticipating?

- Have some extra slides ready.
- Decide in advance which slides you can skip if running short of time.

6.4.5 Do not answer questions; make participants use the plan

- Direct questions back to participants (rephrasing if necessary).
- Refer them back to the plan.
- If a group is truly stuck:
  - Offer more information.
  - Suggest appropriate tools and techniques.

- Beware of giving deceptive clues to divert attention from items of significance.

6.4.6 Give participants the chance to be self-critical in the debrief

- What went wrong – why?
- What went well – why?
- What can be done better – how?
- Who is responsible for changes – by when?

On completion, chat through with support staff and write up your notes/provisional findings.

6.4.7 Supporting materials

Any mocked-up press articles or pictures that can bring the scenario to life should be used where possible. Make sure that all the injects are accurate, for example, the correct police force; a common error in London is a failure to distinguish between the Met and the City Police.

6.4.8 Post-exercise report

Ideally the post-exercise report should be published soon after the exercise so as to maintain the enthusiasm for improvement. The formats of reports are myriad but the common features include:

- Introduction
- Executive summary
- Aim and objectives
- Planning and preparation (key tenets of the exercise cycle – who was consulted with in the research phase)
- Participants
- Delivery (format)
- Annex A: Findings and recommendations against the aim and objectives
- Annex B: Main events list for future reference

6.4.9 Scenario advice and options

Scenarios are one of the most difficult things to devise if they are to capture the imagination of the participants. There are three main issues to contend with, all of which are interrelated.

The level of the exercise

The first is the level of the participants. A strategic-level exercise has to deal with strategic issues and the detail is not to be found easily in so far as the strategic group should not be interested in the 'detail' of what has happened, they should be more interested in the position of the firm in the wider environment and the issues for the future. In contrast a facilities-related issue has the need for potentially a plethora of detail so that the plan can really be tested.

The content of the exercise

Content needs to be accurate and relevant, unless it is a deliberate trap to see if participants are diverted by irrelevancies. This type of information is usually found in the BIA and can be used to populate the exercise content. For example, if the time-keeping system is essential, then can it really be used from a remote location?

Often in trying to identify a scenario the author will use broad-brush issues such as a pandemic which, unless carefully tailored to be specific (e.g. all of the IT helpdesk are ill at the same time), will miss the point.

Scenario first or issues first?

It is easier to ask what issues are to be examined by the exercise and then to see what sort of scenario can probe such issues. For example, an issue for Finance might be to ascertain whether they can set up a cost code for all incident-related costs thereby isolating them from normal costs so that the insurers and loss adjusters can settle more quickly. A fire or flood scenario may explore this issue but so would catastrophic IT failure.

6.5 Top tips

6.5.1 Blame

Nobody likes to be blamed for an event either in an exercise or in fact. So try to make the cause of the scenario external to the practice. For example, if the exercise is to focus on IT failures, make the scenario one where the local authority road crew cut the cable to the building.

6.5.2 Something for everyone

Make sure that whatever scenario used has an element of complexity and works for all parties. You might have to be a bit unrealistic on this issue so as to maintain the interest of all participants, but with some thought it can be done.

6.5.3 Unexpected elements

It is often interesting, especially at the management levels where decision-making skills are important, to include an unexpected element or action. This should be designed to challenge them. They should of course maintain focus but it is useful to see how and why they might shift attention from the important to the mundane; it is a good lesson to bring up in debriefs.

6.5.4 Some useful scenario topics

These may include:

- Demonstrators gaining access to the building. It could be a local issue if it is a small firm, for example local 'Fathers for Justice'.
- Data loss and/or compromise howsoever caused. Lawyers can be a prime target for hackers especially if some of the practice's work is in any way financially sensitive or it could be as simple as the theft of a partner's laptop or memory stick.
- Inappropriately acquired matter by a member of staff. Any conflict of interest, compliance and regulatory issue or unforeseen risk can work.
- Arrest of a senior member of the practice. It does happen and it could be made worse if it occurs abroad on a client-related matter.
- Food poisoning of a critical group of staff. This can be used even where there is no canteen, if the staff all go to the same sandwich shop for lunch.
- Air conditioning faults and related server issues.
- Social networking leaks of a personal nature.
- Regional transport infrastructure failure.
- Loss of access to banking systems.
- Internal fraud by a former employee.
- Severing network cables or loss of water supplies caused by the local council.
- Loss of a major client.
- Fire in another part of a shared occupancy building.
- Tower cranes on neighbouring building sites falling over.

Annex 6A

Exercise self-assessment tool

Group	Experience	Environment: weather, location	Emergency services	External clients, etc.	Infra-structure: road/rail, etc.	Third parties: suppliers, contractors	Legal: litigation	Complexity of the issues	Media: TV, social, print	Other issues
	High, medium, low	Hard, moderate, low	All, police, fire, ambulance, none	All, some, none	Bad, partial, normal	All, some, none	Serious, passed	High, medium, low	Inter-national, national, local	Long-, medium-, short-term
Gold	High	Moderate	None	Some	Partial	All	Serious	High	National	Medium
Secretariat	High	Moderate	None	Some	Partial	All	NA	Medium	NA	NA
Silver	Low	Moderate	None	None	Partial	Some	Passed	Low	Local	Short
Silver Admin	Medium	Moderate	None	None	Partial	Some	NA	Medium	NA	NA
Bronze										
HR										
Media										
IT										
Finance										
Operations										
Others										

Annex 6B

Master events list

No.	Time/exercise time	From/to	Inject or serial	Expected actions in plan	Remarks
1	10.00 hrs	Telephone call cascade from police to Facilities Management	Please take all staff to a place of safety as high up in the building as possible and switch off all AC units as there has been a chemical leak at the nearby motorway junction	Internal tannoy to move to invacuation point	If another way of alerting staff is done it is to be noted and logged in detail
2	10.30 hrs	Update from police on radio	The situation will last at least 6 more hours	Open food in location, check medical needs of staff	There are two diabetics on staff and one contractor who may or may not be present

7 Background information

7.1 Emergency services

There are technically four emergency services in the UK: the police, the Fire and Rescue Service, the ambulance service and, for completeness, Her Majesty's Coastguard.

In very brief outline, in relation to a law firm, their roles are as follows.

7.1.1 Police

- Preservation of life.
- Public order.
- For various reasons they tend to assume primacy in a major incident.
- They are not there to secure your law firm if you need additional security.
- In a major incident the police set up a 'casualty bureau'; the purpose of this is to take information from companies about missing staff, they do not tell you if your staff are casualties.
- They communicate with any next of kin: you do not.

7.1.2 Fire and Rescue Service

- Obviously fire fighting and rescuing people.
- 'Plume' modelling and dealing with hazardous chemical leaks.
- They will not put out a fire at your building at significant risk to themselves; remember you are insured. Check your insurance policy for details of coverage, particularly to ensure environmental factors which may affect access are covered. For example, your office may be on the same site as an organisation dealing with hazardous chemicals.
- They will tell you the fire is out; they will not tell you it is OK to go back in the building. You need to get your own building surveyors to check safety issues.

7.1.3 Ambulance service

- They are the portal to the NHS system.
- They 'triage' or grade casualties as to the seriousness of their injuries and get them to hospitals.
- They do not make diagnoses.
- They might have to take some casualties quite a long way in a major incident.
- Do not presume all casualties will be taken to the local hospital which might not even treat casualties.

> **Note:** Most companies take the view that all emergency services' instructions will be obeyed by the workforce and that such instructions override the views of even the most senior partner.

7.2 Armed forces

Despite their recent participation in foot and mouth disease outbreaks, floods, etc., the Armed Forces are not 'emergency services' and should not be relied upon to be involved in any likely event affecting a law firm.

7.3 Miscellaneous reading and websites

Business continuity is inextricably linked to other disciplines and often cannot be dealt with in isolation. We do not expect you to read all these books and websites but here is a selection of what we have found useful in the past.

7.3.1 Business continuity

Publications

Childs, Donna and Dietrich, Stefan, *Contingency Planning and Disaster Recovery: A Small Business Guide*, Wiley, 2002. Useful practical guidance for smaller businesses; particularly good on IT and insurance issues.

Elliott, Dominic, Swartz, Ethné and Herbane, Brahim, *Business Continuity Management: A Crisis Management Approach*, Routledge, 2004. An excellent, concise and very readable explanation of business continuity, situating the discipline in a proper business context. Useful for both BC practitioners and general managers.

Emergency Preparedness: Guidance on Part 1 of the Civil Contingencies Act 2004, its Associated Regulations and Non-statutory Arrangements, HM Government, 2005. Vital reference for organisations covered by the Civil Contingencies Act but also provides useful context for planning private sector business continuity. Available in hard copy from the Cabinet Office Emergency Planning College or on the UK Resilience website (see below).

Hiles, Andrew and Barnes, Peter, *The Definitive Handbook of Business Continuity Management*, Wiley, 2005. Thorough, if rather lengthy, introduction to all aspects of business continuity. Excellent appendix of case studies.

Websites

- Business Continuity Institute (**www.thebci.org**). Useful information on professional standards and development; regulation and standards in the industry; and training and conferences.

- Continuity Central (**www.continuitycentral.com**). Excellent website with wide range of articles on all aspects of BC and weekly updates on BC issues.
- UK Resilience (**www.ukresilience.info**). Government website giving guidance on all aspects of emergency planning.

7.3.2 Risk management

Adams, John, *Risk*, Routledge, 1995. Very interesting exploration of how people and societies understand and (attempt to) manage risk.

Bernstein, Peter L., *Against the Gods: The Remarkable Story of Risk*, Wiley, 1996. Readable and informative account of the development of risk management from Antiquity to the present day.

Chittenden, Jane, *Risk Management Based on M-o-R: A Management Guide*, Van Haren, 2006. Short practical guide to managing risk in line with Office of Government Commerce guidelines.

Dickson, G.C.A. and Hastings, W.J., *Corporate Risk Management*, Witherby & Co, 1989. Concise and readable overview of many aspects of risk management in a corporate context.

Harrington, Scott E. and Niehaus, Gregory, *Risk Management and Insurance*, McGraw-Hill, 2003. Very thorough and interesting exploration of all aspects of the insurance industry.

Martin, Duncan, *Managing Risk in Extreme Environments*, Kogan Page, 2008. By studying risk management in extreme environments (floods, earthquakes, etc.) the author aims to identify risk management lessons applicable to more mundane situations. Contains some excellent case studies.

Oxford Metrica/FM Global, *Improving Risk Quality to Drive Value* (**www. oxfordmetrica.com/pdf/OMRiskQualityreport.pdf**), 2003. Novel research linking good risk management to improved financial performance of companies.

Strategic Risk: A Guide for Directors, Thomas Telford Publishing, 2006. Practical guidance for directors with a particular focus on the construction industry. Sponsored by the Department of Trade and Industry, the Institution of Civil Engineers and the Actuarial Profession. Includes a CD with various presentations and video clips.

Taleb, Nassim Nicholas, *The Black Swan: The Impact of the Highly Improbable*, Allen Lane, 2007. Fascinating exploration of the impact of highly improbable events on all aspects of life.

7.3.3 Crisis management

Bazerman, Max H., *Judgement in Managerial Decision Making*, Wiley, 2006. Excellent exposition of the inherent limitations of our decision-making processes both in normality and in crisis situations.

Bazerman, Max H. and Watkins, Michael D., *Predictable Surprises*, HBS Press, 2004. Useful mixture of psychological theories and practical case studies such as Enron/Arthur Andersen, the failures of aviation security in the US and the overfishing of the North Atlantic.

Borodzicz, Edward P., *Risk, Crisis and Security Management*, Wiley, 2005. A very interesting, but somewhat theoretical, exploration of these interrelated fields. Includes some useful case studies.

Dixon, Norman, *On the Psychology of Military Incompetence*, Pimlico, 1994. Fascinating study of the human causes of military disasters with many useful lessons for more general crisis management.

Fink, Steven, *Crisis Management: Planning for the Inevitable*, iUniverse, 2000. Similar to Regester and Larkin, *Risk Issues and Crisis Management* but slightly broader in scope and some interesting older case studies (originally published in 1986).

Flin, Rhona, *Sitting in the Hot Seat: Leaders and Teams for Critical Incident Management*, Wiley, 1996. Excellent treatment of the psychology of dealing with crises with some interesting insights on major disasters.

Harvard Business Review on Crisis Management, Harvard Business School Press, 2000. A selection of case studies of varying usefulness.

Kirschenbaum, Alan, *Chaos Organisation and Disaster Management*, Marcel Dekker Inc., 2004. Detailed analysis of emergency planning at all levels of Israeli society with many useful observations applicable to more general crisis management.

Larkin, Judy, *Strategic Reputation Risk Management*, Palgrave, 2003. This book picks up where the author's *Risk Issues and Crisis Management* finishes, with further case studies and much more theory. Also looks in detail at corporate social responsibility and other emerging issues.

Mittelstaedt, Robert, *Will Your Next Mistake Be Fatal?*, Financial Times/Prentice Hall, 2004. Another excellent text on crisis management with many interesting case studies.

Regester, Michael and Larkin, Judy, *Risk Issues and Crisis Management: A Casebook of Best Practice*, Institute of Public Relations, 2002. Excellent coverage of the PR issues of crisis management illustrated with numerous cases.

Smith, Denis and Elliott, Dominic, *Key Readings in Crisis Management*, Routledge, 2006. A compilation of many of the most important papers on crisis management from the last 30 years.

7.3.4 Operational risk management

Alexander, Carol (ed.), *Operational Risk: Regulation, Analysis and Management*, FT Prentice Hall, 2003. Detailed and, at times, highly technical discussion of operational risk in the context of the financial services industry with a particular focus on the implementation of BASEL II.

Cruz, Marcelo, *Modeling, Measuring and Hedging Operational Risk*, Wiley, 2003. The classic text on operational risk; requires significant mathematical background.

Financial Times Mastering Risk – Volume 1: Concepts, Prentice Hall, 2001. Useful introduction to the quantitative treatment of risk. Includes a specific section on operational risk.

Financial Times Mastering Risk – Volume 2: Applications, Prentice Hall, 2001. More advanced and technical treatment of the issues discussed in vol. 1 with limited coverage of operational risk.

Lewis, Nigel, *Operational Risk with Excel and VBA*, Wiley, 2004. Very useful and accessible (although requires prior knowledge of VBA) practical guide to building operational risk models; includes a CD with various VBA models.

7.3.5 Security

Briggs, Rachel and Edwards, Charlie, *The Business of Resilience: Corporate Security for the 21st Century*, Demos, 2006. Short report identifying best practice in corporate security departments in large multinationals.

Demkin, Joseph A. (ed.)/American Institute of Architects, *Security Planning and Design: A Guide for Architects and Building Design Professionals*, Wiley, 2004. Despite the subtitle, this book is easily accessible to a general readership. Whilst focusing on building design, it includes much of general use and interest.

Quigley, Kevin M. and Schmidt, Donald L., *Business at Risk: How to Assess, Mitigate and Respond to Terrorist Threats*, Professional Publishing Group, 2002. Possible alternative to Teeples' *Building Corporate Castles*; generally not as useful but much fuller coverage of insurance issues.

Ranum, Marcus J., *The Myth of Homeland Security*, Wiley, 2004. Similar to Schneier, *Beyond Fear*, but more concerned specifically with information security.

Reference Manual to Mitigate Potential Terrorist Attacks Against Buildings (FEMA 426), US Federal Emergency Management Agency (**www.fema.gov**). Comprehensive guide to assessing and mitigating terrorist risks to buildings.

Schneier, Bruce, *Beyond Fear: Thinking Sensibly about Security in an Uncertain World*, Springer-Verlag, 2003. Excellent and very entertaining look at security in the widest general sense.

Schneier, Bruce, *Secrets and Lies: Digital Security in a Networked World*, Wiley, 2004. Accessible introduction to the whole field of information security.

Teeples, Joe, *Building Corporate Castles: Homeland Defense for Business*, 1st Books, 2002. Good practical guide to managing terrorism risk.

7.3.6 Terrorism

Barbash, Tom, *On Top of the World: Cantor Fitzgerald, Howard Lutnick & 9/11*, HarperCollins, 2003. Interesting lessons on handling the media.

Duffy, John, *Triumph Over Tragedy: September 11 and the Rebirth of a Business*, Wiley, 2002. Interesting account of making up a recovery plan post-event.

INTERSEC: The Journal of International Security, Intersec Publishing. Monthly publication giving good coverage of developments in both threat and risk mitigation.

Leikin, Jerrold and McFee, Robin, *Toxico-terrorism: Emergency Response and Clinical Approach to Chemical, Biological and Radiological Agents*, McGraw-Hill Medical, 2007. Detailed and comprehensive coverage of chemical, biological and radiological agents, their effects and treatments by a wide range of subject matter experts.

Precautions to Minimise Effects of a Chemical, Biological, Radiological or Nuclear Event on Buildings and Infrastructure, Office of the Deputy Prime Minister, 2004. Detailed guidance on planning for CBRN incidents.

Reuter, Christoph, *My Life Is a Weapon: A Modern History of Suicide Bombing*, Princeton University Press, 2004. A very readable account of the global evolution of the phenomenon of suicide bombing.

START Global Terrorism Database, National Consortium for the Study of Terrorism and Responses to Terrorism (**www.start.umd.edu/data/gtd/**). Open-source database including information on terrorist events around the world from 1970 to 2004.

Strategic National Guidance: The Decontamination of Buildings and Infrastructure Exposed to Chemical, Biological, Radiological or Nuclear Substances or Material, Office of the Deputy Prime Minister, 2006. Explanation of the roles and responsibilities of emergency services and others in the aftermath of a CBRN incident.

8 Case studies

The following brief case studies are made anonymous for obvious reasons. That they are anonymous does not diminish their important lessons as all the case studies happened to law firms or organisations working in the legal sector.

We have only sought to protect the identity of the organisations and therefore the staff involved.

8.1 Case study 1

The firm had contracted out some core business systems to a third party. It was in the process of changing its supplier. A virus entered the system. Neither party had agreed who had primacy of decision making in such an event. The net result was that the firm had no e-mail for over one week.

8.1.1 Learning point

Ensure that in the strategy and policies any primacy with third parties is agreed in advance and that they are involved in your planning process and rehearsals.

8.2 Case study 2

A firm's water main was cut and remained unrepaired for almost three days. The firm had been trained in its plan some few months previously and despite some superficial inconvenience (forgive the unintended pun) followed its pre-agreed plans. No billable days were lost in the three days.

8.2.1 Learning point

When in doubt follow the plan. All reasonable and obvious risks, even those from third parties, should have been captured in the risk assessment and suitable plans devised, even if it is only working from home.

8.3 Case study 3

A large firm had some IT cabling severed by a third party. It occurred out of hours and caused all e-mail and phone systems to fail. Within 24 hours the firm was fully operational. The firm's exercise some six months previously had been based on almost exactly the same scenario.

8.3.1 Learning point

Try to identify current and probable risks for any exercises. An overly complex scenario involving terrorism will be controlled largely by the emergency services and at least in the initial stage will not really test your plans.

8.4 Case study 4

A firm lost power to a building which was multi-tenanted. For various reasons, none actually the firm's fault, the generator activated but eventually overheated and shut down despite extensive risk analysis and preventative measures and all facilities management acting correctly. The fault was repaired within 24 hours but a large number of fee-earning hours were lost.

8.4.1 Learning point

Sometimes despite all reasonable endeavours a firm can just be unlucky. A level of balance has to be achieved between concern for risk management and paranoia. Take care concerning who is responsible for which elements of a response in a multi-tenanted building, and check generators and/or power supply regularly.

8.5 Case study 5

The reaction of an organisation to an adverse event (the loss of an operating system) was to seek to identify who was to blame for the cause of the incident as opposed to dealing with the causes and recovery. This reaction was a product of the nature of training of some of the senior staff involved.

8.5.1 Learning point

'To a man with a hammer everything looks like a nail.' Generally people react according to training. Therefore make the scenarios and topics of exercises varied and go beyond the 'normal' fire, flood and theft, etc. scenarios. Challenge the way people think about issues and incidents. Do not seek to apportion blame; it will not help and will often be the subject of a later inquiry.

8.6 Case study 6

A firm lost a critical IT system. The strategic group concentrated on the technical issues and the solution, forgetting to maintain contact with clients. The clients took unilateral action in a vacuum of information coming from the firm. The resultant rework and re-establishment of client relations took many weeks to resolve.

8.6.1 Learning point

The senior group should leave the technical solution to those most capable and maintain effective client liaison. Clients are the lifeblood of the firm and while it is easy to become caught up by the solution to the problem, the real issue is maintaining client loyalty.

8.7 Case study 7

An overseas firm had poor IT security protocols and kept backup tapes in an insecure location. It took over three days to run backups whereupon the firm found that it could not recreate the last three days of e-mails.

8.7.1 Learning point

IT staff may not understand the full implications of what they feel is acceptable practice. There is often a lack of understanding between IT staff and other legal and support staff. Try to bridge the gap by asking questions and taking a mixed group through various scenarios.

APPENDIX A
Glossary

Most professions evolve a language of their own (if only to preserve a mystique as to their activities); business continuity is no exception but fortunately the terms are usually just an abbreviation or common sense.

These are some of the terms which you might encounter; know what they mean and you are less likely to be bamboozled by the practitioners of business continuity.

Business continuity acronyms	Full expansion	Definition
App	Application	A piece of software or a program on a server that allows you to do something on your computer
BAU	Business as usual	Usually related to the recovery phase to BAU. Some commentators believe that the business continuity plan should maintain BAU but in reality this is unlikely to be feasible unless your practice has extensive resources to devote to the plan
BCM	Business continuity management	Planning which identifies an organisation's exposure to internal and external threats and its resources and assets to ensure continuity of service
Call cascade	None	A call-out process where one person calls five others who call five others, etc. Often it is now automated on servers with specialist companies
CMT	Crisis Management Team	CMT is used most frequently to describe response teams. Note that 'crisis' has connotations that are not always helpful in PR terms. See also 'Gold, Silver, Bronze'
DC	Data centre	A location in which your data is held off site; ideally there should be two
DR site	Disaster recovery site	An alternative location from which ongoing work can be undertaken. It can include commercially available sites, mutual aid locations within the practice and temporary offices. It is subdivided as follows: • Cold site, i.e. a building with no IT or communications infrastructure • Warm site, a location with appropriate systems that would need activation and transfer • Hot site, a like-for-like replication of the office environment ready at almost no notice

Business continuity acronyms	Full expansion	Definition
Firewall	None	Device or software designed to protect your network from unauthorised access
Gold, Silver, Bronze	See also SCG, IMT and ORT	Used in the emergency services. In essence, Gold teams think and direct, Silver teams translate directives into practical tasks and Bronze teams perform them. The Home Office endorses this system and it is useful to mirror this in practices large enough to warrant such a division of roles
IMT	Incident Management Team	See, e.g. 'Gold, Silver, Bronze'
MEL	Master events list	A script for planning a business continuity awareness exercise which also establishes the success criteria on which the exercise is based
MTPD	Maximum tolerable period of disruption	Time period after which an organisation's viability will be irrevocably threatened if the product or service delivery cannot be resumed
ORT	Operational Response Team	See, e.g. 'Gold, Silver, Bronze'
RPO	Recovery point objective	The point in time to which data have to be recovered in order to resume ICT services
RTO	Recovery time objective	Target time for the resumption of product or service delivery or activity after an incident
Server	None	A computer or series of computers that runs applications, for example there will be an exchange server that runs the Outlook application that lets you send and receive e-mails
SGG	Strategic Control Group	See, e.g. 'Gold, Silver Bronze'
Sitrep	Situation report	A phrase used in emergency services for a structure update. It has several cousins like casrep – casualty report
Triage	None	A process of grading casualties for treatment by the ambulance service
UPS	Uninterrupted power supply	Usually a bank of batteries which allows servers to do a structured power down as opposed to crashing. The batteries will last only 20 mins to 2 hours